Dedication

This book is dedicated to the Almighty God, who has given me the strength and wisdom to undertake this project. Without His guidance, this book would not have been possible.

To my family, who have always been my support system and my source of inspiration. Thank you for your unwavering love and encouragement throughout my life. Your presence in my life has made it all worthwhile.

To my friends, who have stood by me through thick and thin, thank you for your constant support and encouragement. Your friendship has made my life richer and more meaningful.

May this book serve as a source of knowledge and understanding for all who read it. May it help you identify and avoid the dark triad of narcissism, Machiavellianism, and psychopathy. Let us all strive to create a world where empathy, kindness, and compassion prevail.

To Almighty God, family, and friends, thank you for everything.

Sincerely,

"Every villain is a hero in his own mind."

~TOM HIDDLESTON

CONTENTS

Title Page
Copyright
Dedication
Epigraph
Introduction
Preface
Prologue
~ Blank Page ~

Chapter 1:	2
Chapter 2: Narcissism Unmasked	8
Chapter 3: Machiavellianism Unmasked	19
Chapter 4: Psychopathy Unmasked	29
Chapter 5: Vulnerable Dark Triad	39
Chapter 6: Conclusion	62

INTRODUCTION

The Dark Triad: Unmasked - Understanding and Avoiding Narcissism, Machiavellianism, and Psychopathy is a fascinating book that looks into the mysterious realm of the Dark Triad personality characteristics. These personality qualities, which include narcissism, Machiavellianism, and psychopathy, have long been linked to undesirable consequences and destructive conduct.

The author presents a complete analysis of the Dark Triad in this book, shining light on what makes these characters tick and how they work in social, personal, and professional situations. The author delves into the Dark Triad's beginnings, the variables that lead to its evolution, and the influence it may have on people and society as a whole.

The book also provides practical guidance for those looking to avoid falling victim to people with Dark Triad qualities, as well as ways for coping with these people when they do appear. The author presents readers with a comprehensive grasp of the Dark Triad and the skills they need to defend themselves against its harmful impacts, drawing on a plethora of research and real-life examples.

The Dark Triad: Unmasked is a must-read for everyone interested in understanding the complexity of human behavior, whether you're a mental health professional, a victim of Dark Triad abuse, or simply someone interested in understanding the complexities of human behavior. This book will be a great resource for years to come because to its entertaining writing style, smart analysis, and practical guidance.

PREFACE

This book is a culmination of my deep interest and extensive research on the subject of Dark Triad personality traits - Narcissism, Machiavellianism, and Psychopathy. My primary goal in writing this book is to provide a comprehensive understanding of these traits and their potential impact on individuals and society as a whole.

In today's fast-paced and highly competitive world, individuals with Dark Triad traits are increasingly prevalent, and their actions can have far-reaching consequences. Understanding the characteristics of these traits and how they manifest in people's behavior is essential for individuals, families, and society at large.

In this book, I have attempted to present the information in a clear and accessible way, without sacrificing the complexity and nuance of the subject matter. I have also drawn on a variety of sources, including academic research, case studies, and real-world examples, to illustrate the many facets of the Dark Triad.

I hope that this book will be a useful resource for anyone seeking to understand and avoid the negative effects of Dark Triad traits. Whether you are a student, a mental health professional, or simply someone interested in the subject matter, I believe that this book will provide valuable insights and practical advice.

Finally, I would like to express my gratitude to all those who have supported me in the writing of this book. I hope that it will serve as a useful contribution to the ongoing conversation about Dark Triad traits and their impact on individuals and society.

PROLOGUE

We live in a society where certain people seem to have an amazing capacity to charm, manipulate, and deceive others for their personal profit. These people frequently display narcissism, Machiavellianism, and psychopathy, which is known as the "Dark Triad."

As a society, we often glamorize and romanticize these characteristics, portraying them as desirable attributes for success in a variety of sectors. In actuality, however, people who demonstrate these characteristics frequently endanger themselves and those around them.

In this book, I hope to reveal the Dark Triad by delving into the nature of these personality traits and their influence on individuals and society. I present readers with an in-depth overview of each feature and how it manifests in individuals based on considerable study and personal experience.

Furthermore, I provide practical recommendations on how to detect and avoid people who exhibit these characteristics in both personal and professional contexts. It is my goal that by shining a light on the Dark Triad, we

might strive toward a more equitable and compassionate society that prioritizes integrity and compassion over manipulation and self-interest.

Join me on this journey of understanding and learning as we explore the mysteries of the Dark Triad and learn how to defend ourselves and those we love from its evil influence.

~ BLANK PAGE ~

Dark Triad Unmasked:
Understanding and Avoiding Narcissism, Machiavellianism, and Psychopathy

CHAPTER 1:

What is the Dark Triad?

The Dark Triad. Doesn't that seem like some evil secret society? Unfortunately, it's not that cool. In truth, it is a word used to define three undesirable personality traits: narcissism, Machiavellianism, and psychopathy.

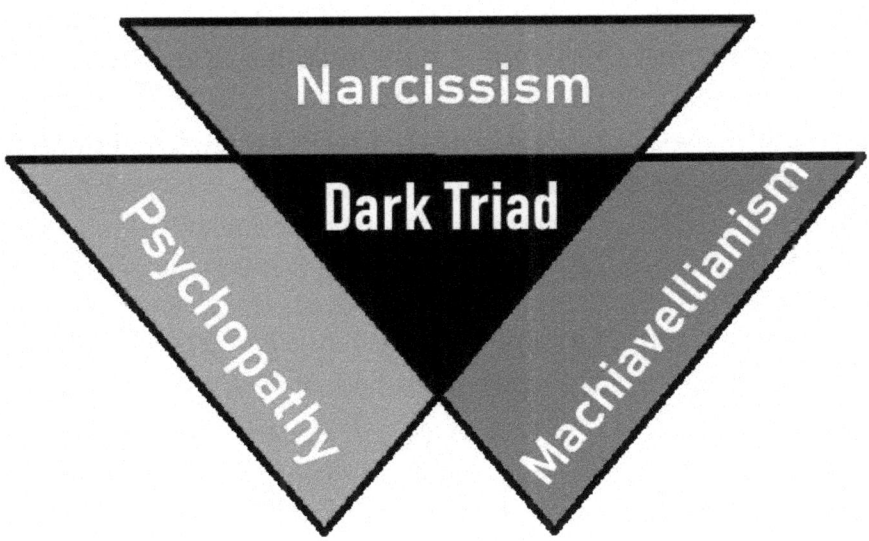

I know what you're thinking. "They sound like wonderful things to have. Sign me up!" Now, before you start purchasing business cards with "Machiavellian Psychopath" as your job title, let's take a deeper look at what these characteristics truly entail.

First and foremost, there is narcissism. When someone has an overinflated feeling of self-importance and a continual desire for adulation, they are suffering from this condition. Essentially, they believe they are hot stuff and want everyone else to believe the same. Then there's Machiavellianism, which is all about deceit and manipulation. Individuals with a high level of this attribute are prepared to go to any length to achieve what they want, even if it means screwing over others in the process. Finally, psychopathy is defined by a lack of empathy and guilt, as well as a proclivity for impulsive action.

I understand what you're thinking. "Yes, these characteristics seem bad, but do they exist in real life?" They, unfortunately, do. Just look at history: many leaders, such as Napoleon Bonaparte and Joseph Stalin, had Dark Triad characteristics. Even today, there are several instances of people that match the category, ranging from some politicians to your sleazy next dooor neighbor.

So don't worry, it's not all doom and gloom. Just because someone has these characteristics does not inevitably make them a villain. On the other hand, simply because someone lacks certain characteristics does not imply that they are a saint. It's vital to remember that everyone is unique and complex, and it's not always simple to fit people into neat little boxes.

Well, there you have it: the Dark Triad. Hey, hey, if you need a Halloween costume, you could always go as a narcissistic, Machiavellian psychopath. So remember to pack plenty of goodies to get others to like you.

Why is it important to understand and avoid it?
Well, the fabled Dark Triad of narcissism, Machiavellianism, and psychopathy. While these characteristics may appear appealing (thanks, Hollywood), they are really extremely damaging in both personal and professional relationships.

Let's dissect it. Narcissism is defined as excessive self-esteem and a lack of empathy for others. Machiavellianism is the use of deceit and manipulation to attain one's objectives. And psychopathy is characterized by a disrespect for the feelings and rights of others, which is frequently accompanied with impulsive and antisocial conduct.

Consider working with someone who exemplifies these characteristics. They will not only be unpleasant to be around, but they may also seriously impair your career and mental health. They may persuade you into doing things you don't want to do or claim credit for your efforts.

Those with Dark Triad qualities can be harsh and dominating in personal relationships. They may deceive you, make you feel insane or overreact, and use your emotions against you.

But, it is not only about defending yourself from others. It's also about recognizing and avoiding these characteristics within oneself. We all have periods of selfishness or manipulation, but when these qualities become dominant, we risk becoming toxic persons who damage those around us.

So, in short, for both personal and professional relationships, it is crucial to recognize and avoid Dark Triad tendencies. It is about safeguarding your well-being and improving who you are. Furthermore, nobody wants to be the bad guy in their own life story.

Overview Of The Book:

The three harmful personality qualities of narcissism, Machiavellianism, and psychopathy are discussed in the book The Dark Triad Unmasked: Understanding and Avoiding Narcissism, Machiavellianism, and Psychopathy. The book offers a thorough examination of the attributes, characteristics, and origins of these dark triad traits, as well as techniques for identifying and averting toxic people and situations. The vulnerable dark triad is a unique form of the standard dark triad that encompasses people who have these features but also experience anxiety, sadness, and poor self-esteem. This issue is covered in the book as well.

The book provides strategies for overcoming these qualities' negative impacts, building wholesome relationships, and fostering emotional and psychological wellbeing. The book's overall goal is to provide readers a thorough grasp of the dark triad and instructions on how to shield oneself against its negative consequences.

~ Blank Page ~

CHAPTER 2: NARCISSISM UNMASKED

What is narcissism?:
The 21st century is plagued by narcissism. Whenever you look, it seems like someone is bragging about themselves, posting selfies, or simply being annoying. So what really is narcissism, and why do certain individuals appear to possess it in abundance? Let's examine this personality attribute in all the detail it merits.

Let's define narcissism first, before anything else. Narcissism is a personality trait that is fundamentally defined by an inflated sense of one's own significance, a lack of empathy for others, and a desire for praise. It resembles having an inflated ego that has taken steroids. Individuals who exhibit narcissistic qualities frequently find it difficult to accept criticism or view situations from another person's point of view because they feel superior to others.

To be sure, there are several types of narcissism. The most well-known kind is undoubtedly grandiose narcissism, which is defined by an excessive sense of one's own importance, a constant yearning for adoration, and a proclivity to exploit others. Moreover, vulnerable narcissism is defined by emotions of vulnerability and fragility, as well as the utilization of attention-seeking actions to mask such feelings. Then there's communal narcissism, which holds that you are better than others because of your moral greatness or selflessness.

So there you have it, a simple explanation of what narcissism is and the various forms you may encounter. Yet, let's face it, we all have a little narcissism in us. After all, who doesn't like a good compliment or a boost to their ego? The goal is to identify when our conduct is out of control and to seek for balance and empathy in our dealings with others.

Signs And Symptoms Of Narcissism:

Ah, narcissists - don't we all know at least one of them? They are the folks who can't stop bragging about themselves, their successes, and their wonderful lifestyles. Is it, however, innocent bragging or something more sinister? Let's look at the indications and symptoms of narcissism.

Exaggerated sense of self-importance:
They have an exaggerated feeling of self-importance and believe they are the center of the universe. As though the entire universe

revolves around them. You know the type: the coworker who interrupts every discussion to brag about themselves, or the buddy who constantly manages to put himself in the spotlight.

Constant need for admiration:

They just can't seem to get enough attention. They'll go to any length to obtain it, from posting numerous selfies on social media to boasting about their achievements at every chance. They're like a thirsty plant that has to be watered all the time, only the water in this case is the admiration of others.

Lack of empathy:

They simply don't understand it, do they? They frequently appear cold or indifferent because they struggle to grasp other people's thoughts or viewpoints. It's as if they're in their own little universe, and everyone else is simply a supporting player in their tale.

Arrogance and entitlement:

They truly believe they are unique, don't they? They feel they are entitled to preferential treatment and benefits simply because they are them. They're the sort of person that cuts in line, wants the best seat in the house, and screams when they don't get their way.

Inability to handle criticism:

Oh boy, this is a big one. They just cannot accept any form of feedback or criticism without taking it personally. It's as if they're wearing a tissue-paper suit, and every unfavorable comment rips it to tears. Because they

can't stand not being flawless, they'll lash out or shut down in reaction.

Manipulative behavior:

Finally, the cherry on top. They will use people to acquire what they want, with little concern for the other person's well-being. It's as if they're playing chess, and everyone else is simply a piece to be moved about the board. They'll lie, cheat, and steal to obtain what they want, then act like they're the hero of the narrative.

I know what you're thinking: "Wow, these guys sound like a lot of fun to be around." And you're not mistaken. Engaging with a narcissist might be like trying to reason with a stone wall. The good news is that there are techniques to shield yourself from their destructive conduct. Thus, the next time you encounter a narcissist, remember that you are in charge and do not have to play their game.

Of course, it's vital to recognize that not everyone who exhibits any of these characteristics is a full-blown narcissist. But, if you see a pattern of these actions in someone, you should proceed with caution.

Causes And Factors That Contribute To The Development Of Narcissism:

Let's get one thing straight - narcissism is more than simply a label for someone who shoots too many selfies. It's a dangerous personality characteristic that may devastate relationships, employment, and general mental wellness. So where does this vexing feature originate from? Let's look at the variables that lead to the development of narcissism.

Childhood Trauma:
Childhood trauma, such as neglect or abuse, might lead to the development of narcissistic tendencies. If a youngster does not get the emotional support they require, they may acquire the feeling that they are unworthy of affection and attention. To compensate, individuals may construct an inflated sense of self-importance in order to maintain their weak self-esteem. It's like a warped superhero origin narrative, only they're not helping anyone; they're just being annoying.

Overindulgence:
Overindulgence is another component that contributes to the development of narcissism. It's natural for someone to acquire a sense of entitlement if they are continuously informed that they are exceptional, gifted, or better than everyone else. They may also struggle with empathy since they are not used to thinking about the needs of others. It's like overfeeding a child and then asking why they grow into a brat.

Media and Celebrity Culture:
The media and celebrity culture may both contribute to the development of narcissism. If a person is continually assaulted with images and messages that celebrate the self and put fame and achievement above all else, it can be difficult to resist the temptation of narcissistic qualities. They may feel they are unique, destined for greatness, or entitled to fame and money. It's like getting sucked into a social media whirlwind and losing touch with reality.

Finally, narcissism is a complicated and multidimensional personality characteristic with major repercussions. While numerous variables contribute to the development of narcissistic tendencies, it is critical to remember that everyone has the ability to choose how they respond to their experiences. Hence, the next time you come across someone with narcissistic characteristics, keep in mind that they may have had a difficult upbringing, been overindulged, or succumbed to media and celebrity culture. They might also be a complete jerk. It might be difficult to tell at times.

How To Avoid Falling Into The Trap Of Narcissism:

The dreaded narcissistic trap. We've all been there, whether it's posting an excessive number of selfies on social media or stopping someone mid-sentence to brag about ourselves. Who doesn't want to be the center of the universe? Yet, my dear reader, it's a trap that's not worth the work.

But don't worry, my dear reader, since I have some advice to assist you avoid slipping into this trap and becoming a full-fledged narcissist.

Practice empathy.

I know, I know. This seems like one of those clichéd self-help advice that you see all the time on Instagram. But hear me out. Empathy is the antidote to narcissism. When you can put yourself in other people's shoes and truly comprehend how they feel, you are less likely to be self-centered and insensitive. Also, empathy is a valuable talent to have in general.

Assume your pal was just dumped. Instead of encouraging them to "suck it up" or "get over it," attempt to understand how they're feeling. Ask them questions, listen to their replies, and provide assistance. They'll enjoy it, I promise.

Surround yourself with honest people.

You can never grow as a person if you only associate with individuals who tell you what you want to hear. You need pals who will call you out when you're being a jerk. And, let's be honest, we've all been jerks at some point in our lives. The idea is to learn from your errors and strive to be better.

Let's assume you're at a party and you're dominating the discussion. Your pal approaches you and says, "Hey, you're kind of dominating the conversation. Can you allow other individuals to speak as well?" Instead of becoming defensive, take their remarks to heart and strive to be more observant in the future.Stay humble. This one is tough, especially if you've had some success in your life. But it's important to remember that you're not the only person in the world. There are billions of people out there, and each one is just as important as you are. Keep your ego in check and remember that you're not invincible.

Be open to criticism.

This one is challenging as well, but it's essential if you want to stay away from being a narcissist. Everyone may need some development; nobody is flawless. When someone criticizes you, accept it graciously and see it as a chance to improve.

Take the following scenario: You are working on a project, and your employer gives you some input. Listen to what they have to say rather than defending yourself or coming up with an explanation, then attempt to put their advice into practice.

Practice gratitude.

Lastly, if you want to stay away from being a narcissist, you must cultivate thankfulness. Consider what you do have for a minute rather than always dwelling on what you lack. You may develop a sense of happiness and lessen your desire for continual approval by engaging in acts of appreciation.

Let's take the scenario where you are depressed over not being able to buy a gorgeous new automobile. Spend some time appreciating the things you do have, such as your health, your family, and your friends, rather than constantly thinking about what you don't have.

So there you have it. You may avoid sliding into the narcissistic trap by cultivating empathy, associating with truthful people, being modest, being open to criticism, and cultivating thankfulness. You don't want to fall into that trap, I can assure you of that. And if all else fails, simply keep in mind the adage, "It's not the size of your ego that matters, it's how you use it."

~ Blank Page ~

CHAPTER 3: MACHIAVELLIANISM UNMASKED

What is Machiavellianism?
Well, Machiavellianism, the devious, cunning cousin of narcissism from the evil triad. You know, the person who usually concocts a scheme in secret and waits for the ideal opportunity to strike? It is machiavellian thinking, I agree.

What precisely is it, then? It's a personality trait that is defined by slyness, deceit, and a priority on one's own interests. To put it another way, Machiavellians believe in using all means necessary to further their own interests, regardless of the costs to others.

Some Warning Signs And Symptoms Of Machiavellianism Are As Follows:

Ruthlessness:

Machiavellians will do whatever it takes to succeed. They don't have a problem exploiting and dumping individuals as they go. You believed you were their buddy, right? Reconsider your position. You are only a piece in their chess game.

For instance, do you recall how your Manipulative coworker won your friendship and persuaded you to divulge your creative concepts for the major project? and then at the meeting claimed all the glory for them? Indeed, it is brutal.

Manipulation:

Machiavellians are experts in trickery and deception. They know exactly how to communicate to obtain what they want, and they will employ whatever strategy required to make their objectives a reality. Nothing they say should be taken at face value since it is almost certainly a lie.

Example: Your Machiavellian ex-partner made you the most incredible promises before stealing all of your money. Classic deception.

Strategic thinking:

Machiavellians are always thinking many steps ahead, calculating their next move. They plan every move as chess players do to keep one step ahead of the competition.

Example: Your Machiavellian employer understood just how to manipulate you into working unpaid overtime. They then handed their preferred minion the promotion. Great strategy.

Lack of empathy:

In order to advance, Machiavellians don't care who they harm or walk on. They lack all empathy for others; they're like heartless machines.

Example: Knowing full well that you had a job the next day, your Machiavellian neighbor held a crazy party at 3 am on a workday. Who gives a damn about the sentiments of others, after all?

Self-centeredness:

The self-centeredness of Machiavellians is astounding. They consider themselves to be the center of the universe, with everyone else existing to fulfill their demands. They are frequently haughty and entitled, and they have an exaggerated feeling of their own significance.

You could be asking yourself, "Wait, aren't being cunning and strategic advantageous in some circumstances?" Yes and no, I suppose. Machiavellianism can be a successful tactic in some situations, but it frequently comes with a high price, such as ruined relationships and a damaged reputation.

Consider the scenario where you are competing with a coworker for a promotion at work and you are aware that they both want the same job. A Machiavellian strategy can entail undermining your coworker's efforts or fabricating unfavorable stories about them in order to make oneself appear superior in contrast. Yet at what price? By alienating your coworker and other employees, you run the risk of developing a bad reputation as a manipulative and unreliable person.

Hence, even if Machiavellianism could appear like a seductive shortcut to success, it's crucial to consider the possible repercussions before using Machiavellian techniques.

Causes And Factors That Contribute To The Development Of Machiavellianism:

Let us now discuss the diabolical trait of Machiavellianism. If you've met someone who is deceptive, cunning, and ruthless, you've probably met a Machiavellian. So how can someone develop like this? Let us look at some of the causes and elements that have contributed to the rise of Machiavellianism:

Parental Influence:
It's no wonder that your parents influenced your Machiavellian inclinations. Did your mother or father employ manipulative methods or demonstrate symptoms of being a master of deception and lies? Well, congratulations! You are now a product of your parents' upbringing. Those who grow up with such parents are more prone to develop Machiavellian qualities themselves, according to research. It's similar to a family inheritance, however instead of silver spoons, it's a silver tongue that can persuade others into doing what you desire.

Environment:
Being raised in a toxic atmosphere where individuals are continually lying, deceiving, and manipulating can also help to shape Machiavellianism. For example, if you grew up in a family where everyone was always arguing and trying to get their way by any means possible, it may have rubbed off on you. Congrats, you have officially become the person in your family who you despise the most.

Personal Experiences:
Have you encountered severe trauma or betrayal in your life? It's

no surprise, then, that you developed Machiavellian inclinations. When someone injure you, it's natural to want to defend oneself at any costs, which sometimes includes resorting to deceptive techniques. "Hurt people hurt people," as they say.

Success Orientation:
Ah, the ultimate motivators for Machiavellian behavior: power and achievement. People that are very competitive and determined may use Machiavellian strategies to advance. They feel that the purpose justifies the means and that nothing can stop them from succeeding. Why not? It's just business, right?

These Are Some Examples To Help You Spot Machiavellian Behavior In Others:

A person who grew up with a domineering and manipulative mother may have learnt to manipulate others to get their way.

Someone who grew up in a home where lying and cheating were common may have learnt that those activities are acceptable, even necessary, in order to obtain what they want.

A person who has been the victim of a big betrayal may resort to Machiavellian measures to shield themselves from future harm.

A highly competitive company leader may employ Machiavellian strategies to remove competitors and obtain a promotion or agreement.

"Well, I'm not a Machiavellian, so why should I care?" you might be thinking. The fact is that we all meet people with these characteristics at some time in our life. As a result, it's critical to understand the origins and elements that lead to Machiavellianism so that we may better defend ourselves against people who would employ these techniques against us. After all, being forewarned is being forearmed!

How Can We Prevent Falling Into Machiavellianism's Trap:

What is the polar opposite of a Machiavellian? A person who falls victim to Machiavellianism! Why add to the world's already-heavy dose of deception and manipulation? To prevent becoming a Machiavellian, follow these strategies and tactics to stay loyal to yourself and avoid slipping into the trap of Machiavellianism:

Be honest with yourself.
Understand your values, beliefs, and limitations. You will be able to make judgments based on what you believe is correct rather than what others believe.

Empathize with others - Put yourself in the shoes of others and try to understand their perspective. This will assist you in making choices that benefit other people as well as yourself.

Be open and transparent.

While interacting with people, avoid from being secretive or deceptive. Being truthful and open in your conversation may promote respect and trust.

Don't use others for personal gain.

Don't use or manipulate people for your personal gain. Work cooperatively with others to accomplish shared objectives instead.

Be accountable for your actions.

Admit your mistakes, offer an apology if needed, and try to make things right. In addition to mending relationships, this can help establish trust.

Keep in mind that Machiavellianism is not a good trait, and that slipping into its trap can have detrimental effects on both you and people around you. You may avoid slipping into the trap of Machiavellianism and have a constructive effect in both your personal and professional lives by being honest, empathic, transparent, courteous, and accountable.

And keep in mind that karma is a b*tch if you ever feel inclined to channel your inner Machiavellian.

~ Blank Page ~

CHAPTER 4: PSYCHOPATHY UNMASKED

What is psychopathy?
Psychopathy is a personality disorder characterized by a pattern of persistent antisocial conduct, poor empathy and regret, and brash, disinhibited, and egocentric characteristics. It's a disorder that may be quite distressing for those around the affected individual, and it's regrettably more frequent than we'd like to acknowledge.

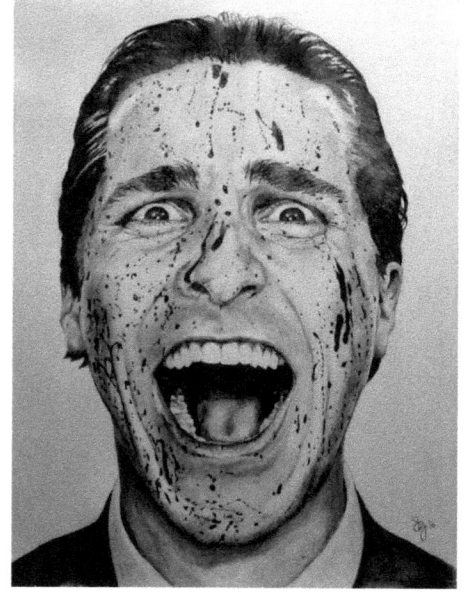

While some psychopaths may be able to thrive in society without ever being arrested for their illegal acts, others may wind up in jail or other institutions. Psychopathy treatment is tough because psychopaths are resistant to change and may not respond to regular psychotherapy or medication. Certain modern therapies, including as cognitive-behavioral therapy and mindfulness-based interventions, may, nevertheless, show promise in helping people with psychopathy manage their symptoms and enhance their quality of life.

These Are Some Instances That Will Help You Recognize Psychopaths:

Ted Bundy

Ted Bundy was one of history's most iconic serial killers, and for good cause. He was responsible for the murders of at least 30 young women in the 1970s, and he had a total lack of empathy for his victims. He was notorious for his attractive and captivating nature, which he used to get his victims into his automobile before attacking and killing them. His crimes were marked by great violence and cruelty, with some victims sexually raped and disfigured after death. At his trial, Bundy's psychopathic characteristics were on full display, as he displayed no remorse for his conduct and even functioned as his own defense counsel.

Jordan Belfort

Jordan Belfort is a former stockbroker who rose to prominence in the 1990s for his part in scamming investors out of millions of dollars. He was well-known for his lavish lifestyle, which included parties, drugs, and flashy automobiles. Belfort's seductive personality and exaggerated feeling of self-importance were critical elements in his ability to deceive and swindle his clients. Despite being apprehended and sentenced to jail for his crimes, Belfort has used his celebrity to his advantage, penning a biography that was eventually made into the film "The Wolf of Wall Street," starring Leonardo DiCaprio.

Patrick Bateman

Patrick Bateman is the primary character in the novel "American Psycho," which was subsequently made into a film starring Christian Bale. Bateman is a successful investment banker who also happens to be a serial killer. He is cold, calculating, and displays no emotion for his victims. Bateman's psychopathic tendencies are demonstrated by his fascination with material items, readiness to perpetrate horrible acts of violence, and delusions of grandeur. Despite his misdeeds, Bateman is able to maintain a veneer of normalcy in his career and social life, making him a disturbing illustration of the potential threat offered by persons with psychopathic qualities.

These examples serve as a reminder that psychopathy is more than simply a theoretical term; it can have real-world implications. Understanding the qualities and actions linked with psychopathy allows us to better protect ourselves and others from people who may constitute a threat.

Ultimately, psychopathy is a complicated and troublesome disorder. It's crucial to realize that not everyone who shows these characteristics is a psychopath, and that psychopathy is an uncommon disorder. But, it is equally critical to be aware of the indications and symptoms of psychopathy in order to protect yourself from individuals who may be manipulating or using you.

Signs And Symptoms Of Psychopathy:

Alright, let's dive into the details of psychopathy.

Lack of Empathy:
This is one of the most noticeable characteristics of psychopathy. Individuals who exhibit psychopathic characteristics have little to no empathy for others. They are unconcerned with other people's feelings, ideas, or needs. They can be oblivious to the suffering of others and may even love inflicting misery. Their lack of empathy enables them to control and exploit people without regret or shame.

Impulsivity:
Impulsive behavior is a hallmark of psychopaths. They take action without considering the effects of their choices. They might only consider their own immediate wants or interests while making decisions, paying little attention to how their choices might influence other people. Because of their impulsivity, they might be unpredictable and dangerous since they may behave violently or

criminally without provocation.

Manipulative Behavior:
Psychopaths are masters at manipulation. They utilize their charm and charisma to achieve what they want from others, frequently without the other person noticing. They may lie, cheat, or deceive people to attain their aims, and they rarely feel sorry about it. They have a way of making individuals feel unique and important, just to dump them after they've fulfilled their purpose.

Criminal Behavior:
It's not surprising that psychopaths are more prone than the wider population to commit crimes. Both the law and societal conventions are disregarded by them. Without feeling guilty or regret, they may commit violent crimes, theft, or fraud. They could believe they are above the law, and they might even find the pleasure of breaking the law and getting away with it thrilling.

Common Traits:
Some personality features linked to the disorder are frequently displayed by psychopaths. They could be overconfident in themselves and think they are superior to others. They could have a haughty attitude toward others and be conceited toward themselves. In addition to lacking empathy, as we've already said, they could also be superficially charming and capable of controlling people.

Causes And Factors That Contribute To The Development Of Psychopathy:

We've all met someone who appears to be devoid of emotion and guilt, and who radiates a charm that seems too good to be true. The individual might be a psychopath.

Let's now look at some instances where these elements may have an impact on the emergence of psychopathy:

Genetic predisposition:

Let's imagine your dad is a cutthroat and emotionless businessman with a successful track record. You receive his genes, which increase your propensity to becoming psychotic. You also learn to admire him and model your conduct after him as a child, which can help to normalize and promote psychopathic traits.

Childhood trauma:
Consider yourself a youngster who is subjected to physical abuse by your parents. In order to live, you learn to repress your feelings and separate yourself from your suffering. This emotional distance develops into a habit as you age, which helps you deal with challenging circumstances. It also makes it more difficult for you to grasp the effects of your actions on other people and sympathize with them.

Brain abnormalities:
Let's imagine you have a smaller amygdala than the majority of individuals have. As a result, you are less prone to get fearful and anxious when confronted with potentially hazardous situations.

You're also less prone to experience regret or guilt for hurting someone else. As a result, you could take risks without thinking about the effects they might have on you or other people.

So there you have it: a few of the reasons and elements that play a role in the emergence of psychopathy. It's a challenging and fascinating subject that has interested both academics and the general public. Yet, let's not overlook the negative effects of psychopathic conduct in daily life and the need of being aware of it in ourselves and others.

How To Avoid Falling Into The Trap Of Psychopathy:

Let's delve deeper into each of these:

Hey, we all have some strange inclinations and behaviors that we're not proud of. Recognize problematic patterns. But it's time to examine more closely if you start to see behavioral patterns that are routinely damaging to other people or to yourself. Perhaps you have a propensity for losing control when you're angry, or perhaps you lie and manipulate frequently to achieve your goals. Whatever it is, don't punish yourself for it; instead, accept it and make an effort to change it.

Build Healthy Relationships.

It's not about having a lot of friends, as they say; it's about having good friends. Furthermore, excellence is essential if you want to stay away from being a psychopath. Focus on developing real, supporting ties with individuals who actually care about you rather than looking for superficial connections based on control and power. We assure you that it will provide you much greater satisfaction than attempting to control everyone else.

Avoid Power Struggles.

Ah, power. The ultimate temptation. Power battles are like quicksand, however, so here's the problem. You fall deeper the more you struggle to overcome them. Hence, put more effort into fostering mutual respect and teamwork rather than trying to show people who is in charge. We assure you that in the long term, it is far more fruitful (and less stressful).

Seek Professional Help.

Seeking assistance when you need it is not a sign of weakness. And if you're worried that you could possess psychopathic traits, it's crucial to consult a specialist who can assist you in resolving your problems.

There are several services available to assist you in avoiding slipping into the psychopathy trap, including therapists, mental health professionals, and support groups. And let's face it, who doesn't enjoy working with a competent therapist?

Do not assume that simply because you show signs of psychopathy, you will eventually develop into a full-blown psychopath. You can stay out of the trap and have a happy, healthy life with a little self-awareness and effort.

~ Blank Page ~

CHAPTER 5: VULNERABLE DARK TRIAD

What is the vulnerable dark triad?
Let me tell you, it's similar to the traditional dark triad but with a twist. It's similar to that beloved classic film you adore, but with an additional hour of omitted scenes—not necessarily a good thing, my friend.

Let's simplify it so that it can be understood by even the most egotistical, Machiavellian, and psychotic individuals.

What is the vulnerable dark triad?
It's a division of the dark triad made up of people who exhibit narcissistic, Machiavellian, and psychopathic traits as well as anxiety, sadness, and poor self-esteem. Talk about getting hit twice.

The great desire for praise and validation from others that frequently characterizes persons with the vulnerable dark triad can make them even more cunning and deceptive than those with the classic dark triad.

Also, compared to those without dark triad qualities, they could be more prone to self-harm and suicide thoughts.

How is it different from the traditional dark triad?

The vulnerable dark triad is characterized by a deep-seated fear of being rejected and failing, whereas people with the typical dark triad are frequently self-assured and confident.

They may act even more irrationally out of fear to shield their frail egos, including lying, cheating, and manipulating others.

Because it frequently goes unnoticed and people conceal their fears with their dark triad features, the vulnerable dark triad can be much more sneaky and harmful than the typical dark triad.

Examples Of The Vulnerable Dark Triad:

A manager who battles with thoughts of worthlessness and inadequacy while simultaneously continuously belittling and undermining their staff in an effort to feel superior.

A dominating and possessive love partner who also harbors a strong fear of being dumped or rejected.

A close friend who likes to dominate talks and be the focus of attention while simultaneously seeking approval from others.

Similar to the dark triad but carrying more emotional weight is the vulnerable dark triad. Just because someone appears certain and in charge on the outside doesn't imply they aren't battling their own inner issues.

Where Dark Triad fits into the other personality models.

Examining how the Dark Triad relates to the Big Five personality traits is one method to analyze how it differs from other personality models. Openness, conscientiousness, extraversion, agreeableness, and neuroticism are the five main aspects that make up the commonly used "Big Five" personality paradigm.

According to research, the Big Five feature of agreeableness and the Dark Triad qualities are negatively associated, therefore those who score highly on the Dark Triad tend to score poorly on agreeableness. Given that people who display the Dark Triad qualities are typically more concerned with their own interests than those of others, this makes sense.

Narcissism is favorably connected with extraversion and negatively correlated with neuroticism, whereas Machiavellianism is adversely correlated with agreeableness and conscientiousness, according to research on the other Big Five qualities. Moreover, conscientiousness and agreeableness are adversely linked with psychopathy.

The Dark Triad and the Big Five so have different characteristics, but they also have obvious connections. The Dark Triad, in particular, exhibits a lack of empathy and a preoccupation with self-interest, whereas the Big Five offers a more comprehensive framework for comprehending personality across various dimensions.It's also important to note that several different personality models have been connected to the Dark Triad. For instance, it has been discovered that the sixth dimension of honesty-humility—which is part of the HEXACO model of personality—is adversely connected with the Dark Triad. In contrast to people who score well on the Dark Triad, those who score highly on honesty-humility are more likely to be truthful, humble, and fair-minded.

In conclusion, the Dark Triad personality qualities are distinct from those of other personality models, such as the Big Five, but there are also obvious connections between the Dark Triad and other personality dimensions. These connections aid in our comprehension of how personality is structured and how various qualities interact with one another.

Is there any correlation between Dark triad and Generation Me?

The term "Generation Me" refers to a group of people who identify as individualistic, self-absorbed, and entitled, and who were born between the early 1980s and late 1990s. The Dark Triad, a group of psychological characteristics that includes narcissism, Machiavellianism, and psychopathy, has been reported to have some qualities that are also present in this generation. In this paper, the connection between Generation Me and the Dark Triad will be examined, along with some possible explanations.

It's crucial to define the term "Generation Me" at the outset. Many social, economic, and technical developments, such as the emergence of social media, globalization, and the growing focus on individual accomplishment have influenced this generation. As a result, compared to earlier generations, people of this age are frequently more self-centered and possess a stronger feeling of entitlement. Also, they are more inclined to prefer short-term goals over long-term ones and to value immediate satisfaction above social duty.

So, how do the Dark Triad and Generation Me relate to one another? There is a chance that the social and cultural influences that have created this generation have also influenced how the Dark Triad has evolved. Because it is now simpler than ever to build and manage a personal brand on social media, for instance, narcissistic tendencies may be exacerbated. Similar to this, a focus on success and personal achievement can promote a Machiavellian mentality in which the objectives justify the methods. Lastly, impulsive conduct and a lack of empathy may be exacerbated by the emphasis on rapid satisfaction.

Another possibility is that the relationship between Generation Me and the Dark Triad is more complex. While there may be some overlap between these two concepts, it is important to note that not all members of Generation Me display Dark Triad traits, and not all people who score high on Dark Triad traits belong to Generation Me. Furthermore, there are likely to be other factors that contribute to the development of these traits, such as genetics and early childhood experiences.

It's also possible that the connections between Generation Me and the Dark Triad are more complicated. Although there may be some similarities between these two ideas, it is vital to keep in mind that not all members of Generation Me exhibit Dark Triad qualities, and not all individuals with high Dark Triad trait scores are members of Generation Me. In addition, it's possible that additional elements, including genetics and early life experiences, also have a role in the development of these characteristics.

There has been some studies on the correlation between gender, race, and the Dark Triad, but the results weren't always consistent.

Is there any correlation between the Dark Triad and Gender?

Men regularly show more affiilliation to the Dark Triad traits than women, according to research. In a meta-analysis of over 40 research, for instance, it was discovered that men were more likely than women to exhibit narcissism, Machiavellianism, and psychopathy (Grijalva et al., 2015). According to a different research, males outperformed women in terms of subclinical psychopathy but not narcissism or Machiavellianism (Jonason et al., 2015). Although it is unclear why males tend to score higher on the Dark Triad qualities, some studies have hypothesized that gender roles and cultural expectations may be at play.

Is there any correlation the dark Triad and Race:

On the relationship between race and the Dark Triad qualities, very few studies have been conducted, and the findings are inconsistent. Many studies have found that some racial or ethnic groupings score higher on particular Dark Triad qualities. One research, for example, found that subclinical psychopathy was one area where African Americans outperformed White Americans, but not narcissism or Machiavellianism (Murphy et al., 2016). Asian Americans did lower than European Americans in a different study's assessment of their comprehension of Machiavellianism (Tang & Richardson, 2014).

Yet, other research has not shown any discernible variations in Dark Triad characteristics between racial or ethnic groupings. For instance, one study found no observable differences in any of the Dark Triad characteristics between African Americans and White Americans (Kosson et al., 2016). Similar to this, another study found no observable differences in any of the Dark Triad traits between Hispanic and non-Hispanic respondents (Curtis & Buss, 2019).

It is crucial to keep in mind that many factors, including cultural and environmental ones, can influence personality traits. As a result, it might be difficult to extrapolate general generalizations about how race, gender, and the Dark Triad are related from research findings. Further research is necessary to fully understand the complex relationships between these elements.

Quick Test to find likeliness for Dark triad:

Note: A total score of more than 70 suggests a higher likelihood of possessing characteristics associated with the dark triad.

The dark triad cannot be tested clinically with this test; it is just suggestive. Contact a physician or psychiatrist for greater assistance. (Yes=10, No=0)

1) How much do you agree with the following statement, "I like manipulating others to obtain what I want, even if it harms them?" on a scale of 1 to 10?

2) How often do you feel entitled to special treatment or privileges that others do not receive?

3) Have you ever purposefully lied to someone or used manipulation to get them to think something false?

4) How much do you agree with the following statement: "I am frequently jealous of others and their triumphs, and I may even sabotage them to prevent their success?" Use a scale of 1 to 10.

5) Have you ever purposefully caused emotional or bodily harm to someone just because you wanted to?

6) How frequently do you believe that you are exempt from laws and norms and may act anyway you choose without facing any repercussions?

7) How much do you agree with the following statement: "I like seeing people suffer, and I may even injure them only to observe their pain"? Use a scale of 1 to 10.

8) Have you ever used threats to acquire what you want or to exert control over someone?

9) How frequently do you believe that someone is trying to harm you and that you should defend yourself immediately?

10) How strongly do you agree with the following statement, "I have no qualms about taking advantage of people to attain my aims, even if it harms them?" on a scale of 1 to 10?

The presence of a personality disorder or the Dark Triad features does not necessarily follow from a single response to any one of these questions, it is crucial to remember. To make a diagnosis, a qualified physician would need to carefully examine the patient and take into account a number of variables.

Is Dark Triad traits, leads to affiliation with the far-right groups and engagement in crime?
A group of psychological characteristics known as the Dark Triad includes narcissism, Machiavellianism, and psychopathy. High scorers in these areas are frequently seen as attractive and seductive, but also cunning and dangerous. There is evidence to show that certain Dark Triad persons are drawn to alt-right authoritarianism and are more likely to participate in criminal action, even if not all people who score highly on the Dark Triad qualities do.

The political doctrine known as "alt-right authoritarianism" places a strong emphasis on authoritarianism, nationalism, and frequently white supremacy. This ideology's adherents frequently harbor deep misgivings about liberal democracy and the rule of law and may support using force to further their objectives. Although not all followers of alt-right authoritarianism exhibit the Dark Triad qualities, there is evidence that the two are connected.

The Dark Triad qualities and alt-right authoritarianism's shared emphasis on power and control may be one explanation for this link. Those who belong to the Dark Triad may be lured to this philosophy because it gives them a plan for attaining their objectives through force and deception. Similarly, those who favor alt-right authoritarianism may be drawn to members of the Dark Triad because they are regarded as capable leaders who are not afraid to take drastic measures.

The contempt for others' well-being shared by members of the Dark Triad and alt-right authoritarianism may be another factor in this link. Those who belong to the Dark Triad frequently lack empathy and are eager to take advantage of others. Similar to this, those who embrace alt-right authoritarianism could consider particular groups of people to be inferior or challenges to their authority and be prepared to hurt them in order to achieve their objectives.

There is evidence to show that Dark Triad members may be more inclined to commit cycler crime. The relationship between Dark Triad members and criminal conduct has also been studied. Cycler crime is a phrase used to describe crimes that are done over time repeatedly, frequently going unnoticed. Identity theft, fraud, and cyberstalking are a few examples of crimes committed by cyclists. These kinds of crimes could appeal to Dark Triad members because they let them accomplish their objectives without having to deal with immediate repercussions.

In conclusion, there is evidence that certain Dark Triad persons are lured to the alt-right authoritarianism or criminal conduct, even if not all people who score highly on the Dark Triad features do so. These linkages may be influenced by a common emphasis on control and power, a disdain for other people's well-being, and the possibility of attaining objectives without suffering immediate repercussions. Nonetheless, it's crucial to remember that every person is unique and to avoid generalizing about large groups based on scant evidence.

Signs And How To Recognize And Protect Yourself From The Vulnerable Dark Triad:

Here are some signs to look out for and how to protect yourself from the vulnerable dark triad:

a) Constant desire for affirmation and attention

b Inability to control one's emotions

c) Extreme receptivity to rejection or criticism

d) Tendency to put the blame for their issues on others

e) Impulsiveness and a lack of self-control

f) Unpredictable and inconsistent actions

g) Low self-worth and self-esteem

Healing And Recovery

How to heal and recover from the effects of the Dark Triad:

It can be difficult to heal and recover from the impacts of the Dark Triad, particularly if you've been in a toxic relationship with someone who exhibits these personality qualities. But don't worry, we've got you covered with some useful advice and tactics to support your progress and life reconstruction.

Here are some ways to heal and recover from the effects of the Dark Triad:

Seek Professional Help:

Seeing a psychiatrist or therapist for assistance might be beneficial if you were in a toxic relationship with a person who exhibited symptoms of the Dark Triad. You may get the help and direction you need from a mental health expert to process your feelings and get over any trauma you may have gone through.

Practice Self-Care:

Using self-care as a method to heal and recover from the impacts of the Dark Triad may be quite effective. This might involve things like setting aside time for yourself, participating in interests and hobbies, and surrounding oneself with uplifting and encouraging individuals.

Set Boundaries:

Setting limits is one of the most crucial things you can do to recover from the impacts of the Dark Triad. This entails setting clear limits for what you will and won't accept in your relationships and taking action to uphold those restrictions

Identify and Address Negative Beliefs:

Individuals who have been in relationships with people who exhibit Dark Triad tendencies may come to believe negative things about themselves, such as that they are unlovable or worthless. The first stage in the healing process is to recognize and deal with these false ideas.

Learn from the Experience:

Although going through a toxic relationship can be difficult, it can also be a chance to develop. Spend some time thinking about the lessons you can apply to future relationships based on what you've learned from this one.

Though recovering from the consequences of the Dark Triad requires time and work, it is possible to go ahead and build a better, healthier life for yourself with the correct techniques and assistance.

Strategies For Developing Healthy Relationships And Avoiding Toxic Ones:

Have you ever been stuck in a negative relationship? Maybe you were taken in by their charisma and charm only to discover later that they exemplified the dark triad, whether they were narcissistic, Machiavellian, or psychopathic? Do not be alarmed, my friend, for I have some tactics that can assist you in creating good connections while avoiding those that are harmful.

I can't stand toxic relationships at all. You know the ones I'm talking about—the ones when you feel like you have to continuously be on guard and are unable to do anything. the ones where the demands of the other person are put before your own, leaving you to feel inadequate. It's time to reject that type of foolishness and begin forming wholesome bonds in its place.

To get you started, consider these suggestions:

a) Identifying Toxic Relationships:
Look for behaviors that tend to make you feel anxious or uncomfortable.

Be mindful of how the other person interacts with you and those around them.

If something feels weird, it probably is, so trust your gut.

b) Setting Boundaries:
Clarify your own needs and expectations.

Set boundaries that you can firmly enforce.

When necessary, be prepared to say no, and don't feel bad about it.

c) Communicating Effectively:
Actively consider what the other person is saying while listening.

Employ "I" sentences to convey your feelings.

Don't accuse or criticize the other person; instead, concentrate on coming up with answers together.

d) Building Trust and Respect:
Be sincere and open in all of your dealings.

Keep your word and your promises

Manifest compassion and empathy for the other person's feelings.

e) Practicing Self-Care:
Spend some alone time doing activities you like.

Establish sensible limits for the use of your time and energy.

For the sake of a relationship, don't disregard your physical or emotional health.

Practice active listening:
Rather than using "you" statements, use "I" statements.

Refrain from accusing or criticizing the other person.

Clearly and honestly express your emotions.

Embrace criticism.

In conclusion, it takes work to build good connections and stay away from toxic ones, but the effort is worthwhile in the long term. You may establish trusting and respecting relationships with people by recognizing toxic relationships, setting boundaries, speaking clearly, and engaging in self-care. Therefore, my buddy, go forth and create those wholesome connections!

Self-Care Practices To Promote Emotional And Psychological Well-Being:

Let's speak about self-care techniques that support psychological and emotional health. Because who doesn't need some self-love and care with all the craziness and drama going on around us? The following suggestions can help you feel your best:

Exercise:

I understand that after a hard day dealing with your narcissistic boss, working out is the last thing on your mind. Yet, a decent workout will do wonders for your attitude. Also, if you really push yourself, you may pretend to hit that obnoxious coworker who never stops talking.

Mindfulness:

Let's speak about self-care techniques that support psychological and emotional health. Because who doesn't need some self-love and care with all the craziness and drama going on around us?

The following suggestions can help you feel your best:

Spend a few minutes each day silently sitting and concentrating on your breath. You'll be able to relax and discover some inner peace as a result. Hey, it's also acceptable if your thoughts start to stray and you find yourself plotting your escape from your unpleasant employment.

Gratitude:

Spend some time recognizing your blessings. Just pausing for a moment to express gratitude for your morning cup of coffee or for having a roof over your head can do this. And when your narcissistic ex attempts to reenter your life, simply keep in mind all the reasons you're happy they're no longer in it.

Creativity:

Take part in a creative pastime or endeavor, such as writing, painting, or dance. This might offer you a sense of accomplishment and assist you in healthy emotional expression. And simply tell them it's a new fashion statement if you happen to accidentally spill paint on that white shirt you're wearing to impress your crush.

Self-compassion:

Treat yourself well. Acknowledge that you are putting out your best effort in a challenging circumstance. Moreover, when your inner critic starts telling you that you aren't good enough, tell it to stop talking and take a break.

Keep in mind that caring for oneself is vital, not selfish. So go ahead, give yourself the love and attention you deserve, and put your emotional and psychological well-being first.

~ Blank Page ~

CHAPTER 6: CONCLUSION

We've come to an end of our journey of the narcissist, Machiavellian, and psychopath's dark and treacherous world, people. It's been a crazy trip, let me tell you. We have looked at the qualities, causes, and manifestations of these dark triad personalities, as well as methods for identifying and avoiding toxic people and situations. We've even discussed the vulnerable dark triad, which is the dark triad as a whole but also includes anxiety and poor self-esteem.

But before we say goodbye, let's recap some of the key takeaways from The Dark Triad Unmasked.

a) Awareness is key: You must be aware of the dark triad's presence and how it shows up in people's behaviour if you wish to shield yourself from its damaging effects.

b) Trust your instincts: If something appears strange about a person or a circumstance, pay attention to your

feelings. Often, your intuition will see warning signs before your logical mind.

c) Boundaries are your friend: When interacting with toxic people, setting healthy boundaries is essential. Saying no or avoiding those who make you feel uneasy or unsafe should not be feared.

d) Self-care must always be a top priority: This is especially true while coping with the emotional and psychological repercussions of the dark triad. Whether it's exercise, mindfulness, or artistic expression, choose activities that are effective for you.

e) Healing and recovery from the dark triad's consequences are achievable, even if you were a victim of it. Don't give up hope; instead, ask family members or a mental health professional for help.

I admit that this book may have been a little serious at points, but we also managed to include a few humorous and sarcastic moments. After all, the best medicine is laughing. And who knows, maybe you can take advantage of some of these dark triad characteristics when the circumstances call for it. Just kidding, refrain from doing that.

Genuinely speaking, The Dark Triad Unmasked has given us insightful information and practical advice on how to survive in the world of psychopathy, Machiavellianism, and narcissism. So go forth, my dear readers, and guard yourselves from the poisonous hold of the evil trinity. Remember to summon your inner Beyoncé and tell those poisonous people to "boy bye" if all else fails.

Summary of key points:

The three dangerous personality characteristics of narcissism, Machiavellianism, and psychopathy are explored in the book The Dark Triad Unmasked: Understanding and Avoiding Narcissism, Machiavellianism, and Psychopathy. The book offers a thorough examination of the attributes, characteristics, and causes of these dark triad traits as well as tips for identifying and averting toxic people and situations. The vulnerable dark triad is a special form of the standard dark triad that encompasses people who have these features but also experience anxiety, sadness, and poor self-esteem. This issue is covered in the book as well. The book provides methods for overcoming these qualities' negative impacts, building wholesome relationships, and fostering emotional and psychological wellbeing.

Final thoughts and recommendations:

The Dark Triad Unmasked, in end, is an invaluable tool for anybody who wants to learn more about these perilous personality traits and how they affect people and relationships. The book offers doable methods for identifying and avoiding toxic people, encouraging emotional and psychological wellbeing, and recovering from these qualities' negative impacts.

It is crucial to remember that while the dark triad qualities might be dangerous, not everyone who possesses them is necessarily a nasty person. Some may have underlying mental health difficulties, while some may have developed these habits as coping methods. It's important to approach these people with empathy and comprehension while also safeguarding oneself from any negative actions.

The Dark Triad Unmasked is an insightful and educational book that may assist readers in identifying and avoiding toxic personalities and relationships, fostering emotional and psychological wellness, and eventually leading a better and more satisfying life. Anybody who wants to understand himself and others better should read this book, in my opinion.

~ The End ~

Milton Keynes UK
Ingram Content Group UK Ltd.
UKHW021317171223
434543UK00019B/425